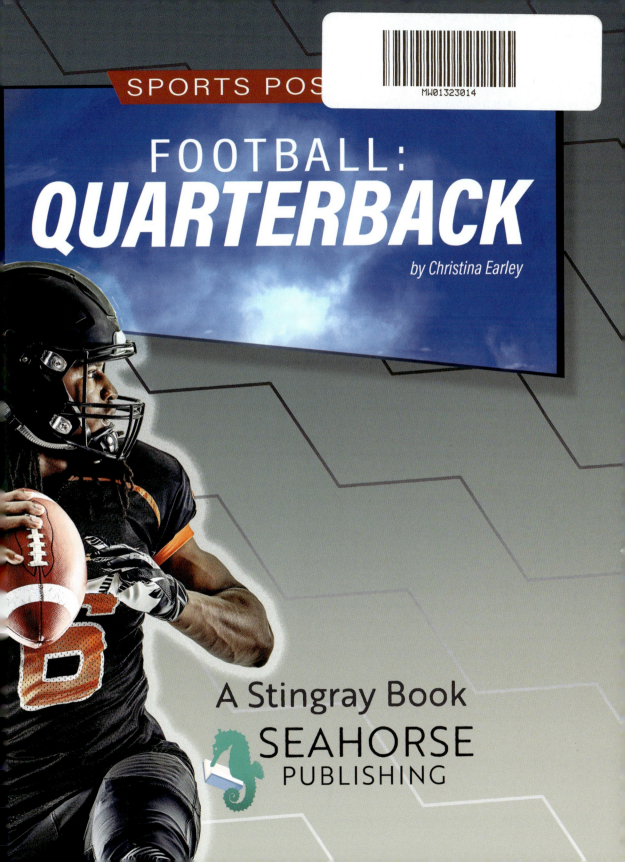

SPORTS POSITIONS

FOOTBALL: QUARTERBACK

by Christina Earley

A Stingray Book

SEAHORSE PUBLISHING

Teaching Tips for Caregivers and Teachers:

This Hi-Lo book features high-interest subject matter that will appeal to all readers in intermediate and middle school grades. It may be enjoyed by students reading at or above grade level as well as by those who are looking for age-appropriate themes matched with a less challenging reading level. Hi-Lo books are ideal for ELL readers, too.

Each book appeals to a striving reader's age and maturity level. Opportunities are provided for students to read words they already know while encountering a limited number of new, high-interest vocabulary words. With these supports in place, students will read more fluently while increasing reading comprehension. Use the following suggestions to help students grow as readers.

- Encourage the student to read independently at home.
- Encourage the student to practice reading aloud.
- Encourage activities that require reading.
- Establish a regular reading time.
- Have the student write questions about what they read.

Teaching Tips for Teachers:

Before Reading

- Ask, "What do I know about this topic?"
- Ask, "What do I want to learn about this topic?"

During Reading

- Ask, "What is the author trying to teach me?"
- Ask, "How is this like something I already know?"

After Reading

- Discuss how the text features (headings, index, etc.) help with understanding the topic.
- Ask, "What interesting or fun fact did you learn?"

TABLE OF CONTENTS

WHAT IS A QUARTERBACK?... 4
UNIFORM... 7
BEFORE THE GAME... 8
DURING THE GAME... 11
TYPES... 12
HISTORY... 15
TRAITS OF A GREAT QUARTERBACK... 16
NOTES FROM THE COACH... 19
G.O.A.T.... 20
GLOSSARY... 22
INDEX... 23
AFTER READING QUESTIONS... 23
ABOUT THE AUTHOR... 24

WHAT IS A QUARTERBACK?

Quarterback is a position on a football team.

Quarterbacks are members of the offensive, or scoring, part of the team.

They are leaders on the field.

Quarterbacks touch the ball on almost every offensive play.

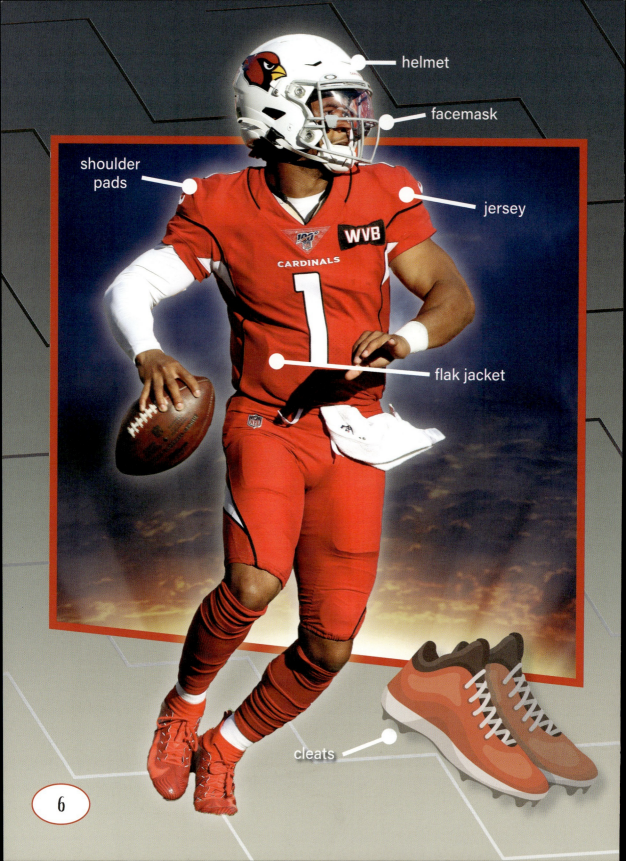

UNIFORM

The shirt of the uniform is a jersey.

Helmets and face masks protect the player's face and head from getting hurt.

Shoulder pads and flak jackets protect the **sternum** and rib cage.

Football cleats give traction on grassy and muddy fields.

FUN FACT
Quarterbacks wear jerseys with numbers from 1 to 19.

BEFORE THE GAME

Quarterbacks practice throwing the ball.

They exercise to get strong.

Some will watch film of games played by their **opponent**.

Eating healthy foods and drinking water help them be ready for game day.

DURING THE GAME

Quarterbacks call the plays in the huddle.

They look to decide if they should throw, pass, or run the ball.

When the **defense** is on the field, some quarterbacks review film of previous plays.

They talk to the coaches and their teammates.

FUN FACT
Wilson has been the exclusive maker of NFL footballs since 1941. They make 4,000 balls every day.

TYPES

The starting quarterback is the player that will be in the game.

The backup quarterback plays if the starting quarterback is injured.

Backups may also hold the ball on placekicks.

Dual-threat quarterbacks are able to run with the ball.

HISTORY

The quarterback position started in the 1800s when Walter Camp changed the rules of **rugby** to make a new game called football.

The name *quarterback* was based on the player's place in the formation.

The job of the quarterback was to hand the ball sideways or backwards to another player.

FUN FACT

In 1934, the shape of the ball was made longer and skinnier. This helped the quarterbacks get a better grip on it.

TRAITS OF A GREAT QUARTERBACK

Quarterbacks have strong arms that can throw a ball with **accuracy**.

They can scan the field quickly to find the open **receiver**.

Staying calm under pressure is important.

To avoid being **tackled**, quarterbacks must be able to move in any direction fast.

FUN FACT

Tom Brady was the 199th player selected in the 2000 NFL Draft. He won his seventh Super Bowl with the Tampa Bay Buccaneers in 2021.

NOTES FROM THE COACH

- Be a leader on and off the field.
- Listen and take constructive criticism from coaches and teammates.
- Admit mistakes and improve.
- Have **grit** to never give up even when things are tough.
- Learn all parts of the game and all positions.
- Work hard during practices and in games.
- Eat a well-balanced diet.
- Have a good attitude and be respectful to others.

G.O.A.T. Greatest of All Time

TROY AIKMAN
College: University of Oklahoma
- Three Super Bowl championships 1993, 1994, 1996
- Six Pro Bowl appearances
- Known as the most accurate passer in NFL history

TOM BRADY
College: University of Michigan
- Seven-time Super Bowl champion 2002, 2004, 2005, 2015, 2017, 2019, 2021
- Five-time Super Bowl MVP 2002, 2004, 20015, 2017, 2021
- Owns 14 Super Bowl records

DREW BREES
College: Purdue University
- Most passing yards in NFL with 80,358 yards
- Super Bowl appearance 2010
- Most passes completed in a career with 7,142 passes

JOHN ELWAY
College: Stanford University
- NFL MVP 1987
- Two-time Super Bowl champion 1998, 1999
- Nine Pro Bowl appearances

BRETT FAVRE
College: The University of Southern Mississippi
- Three-time NFL MVP 1995, 1996, 1997
- Super Bowl win 1996
- Selected NFL First-Team All-Pro three times

PEYTON MANNING

College: University of Tennessee
- Five-time NFL MVP 2003, 2004, 2008, 2009, 2013
- Two-time Super Bowl champion 2007 and 2016
- Seven-time First-Team All-Pro 2003, 2004, 2005, 2008, 2009, 2012, 2013

DAN MARINO

College: University of Pittsburgh
- NFL MVP 1984
- Three-time First-Team All-Pro 1984, 1985, 1986
- Offensive Player of the Year 1984

JOE MONTANA

College: University of Notre Dame
- Two-time NFL MVP 1989, 1990
- Four-time Super Bowl champion 1982, 1985, 1989, 1990
- Three-time First-Team All-Pro 1987, 1989, 1990

AARON RODGERS

College: University California
- Three-time NFL MVP 2011, 2014, 2020
- Super Bowl win 2010
- Three-time All-Pro 2011, 2014, 2020

JOHNNY UNITAS

College: University of Louisville
- Three-time NFL MVP 1959, 1964, 1967
- NFL championships 1958, 1959, 1968, and Super Bowl in 1971
- Five-time First-Team All Pro 1958, 1959, 1964, 1965, 1967

GLOSSARY

accuracy (A·kyoo·ruh·see): precision or correctness

defense (DEE·fens): the team that does not possess the ball who is preventing the offense from scoring

grit (grit): courage and strength of character

opponent (uh·POH·nuhnt): one who competes against or fights another in a contest

receiver (ri·SEE·vuhr): a player who catches the ball when thrown to them

rugby (RUHG·bee): a team game played with an oval ball that may be kicked, carried, and passed from hand to hand

sternum (STUR·nuhm): T-shaped vertical bone that forms the anterior portion of the chest wall

tackled (TA·kuhld): stopped the forward progress of the ball carrier by knocking them to the ground

INDEX

accuracy 16
ball 4, 8, 11, 12, 15, 16
field(s) 4, 7, 11, 16, 19
film 8, 11
game(s) 8, 11, 12, 15, 19
helmets 7
huddle 11
leader(s) 4, 19
offensive 4, 21
teammates 11, 19

AFTER READING QUESTIONS

1. What are dual-threat quarterbacks?
2. What is a good trait for a quarterback?
3. What jersey numbers do quarterbacks wear?

About the Author

Christina Earley lives in sunny Florida with her husband and son. She has always loved different sports. She enjoys traveling to see different stadiums, arenas, and ballparks where she always has to eat the local hot dog.

Written by: Christina Earley
Design by: Kathy Walsh
Editor: Kim Thompson

Photographs/Shutterstock: Cover, Pg 1, 5© STILL is Franck Camhi, Cover, P 3-22 ©ExpressVectors: Cover Pg 5, 6, 9, 10, 11, 14, 17, 18 ©EFKS: P g 6 ©Panda Vector: Pg 6 ©Steve Jacobson: Pg 9 ©wavebreakmedia: Pg 10 ©Ken Durden: Pg 13 ©JoeSAPhotos: Pg 14©Bob Cullinan: Pg 17©Debby Wong: Pg 18©sirtravelalot: Pg 23 ©OSTILL is Franck Camhi

Library of Congress PCN Data
Football: Quarterback / Christina Earley
Sports Positions
ISBN 978-1-63897-103-0 (hard cover)
ISBN 978-1-63897-189-4 (paperback)
ISBN 978-1-63897-275-4 (EPUB)
ISBN 978-1-63897-361-4 (eBook)
Library of Congress Control Number: 2021945214

Printed in the United States of America.

Seahorse Publishing Company
www.seahorsepub.com   1-800-387-7650

Copyright © 2022 **SEAHORSE PUBLISHING COMPANY**

All rights reserved. No part of this publication may be reproduced, stored in a retrieval system or be transmitted in any form or by any means, electronic, mechanical, photocopying, recording, or otherwise, without the prior written permission of Seahorse Publishing Company.

Published in the United States
Seahorse Publishing
PO Box 771325
Coral Springs, FL 33077